Protecting the Homeland

Insights from Army Wargames

Richard Brennan

Prepared for the
United States Army

Approved for public release;
distribution unlimited

RAND
ARROYO CENTER

The research described in this report was sponsored by the United States Army under contract number DASW01-01-C-0003.

Library of Congress Cataloging-in-Publication Data

Brennan, Rick, 1954–
    Protecting the homeland : insights from Army wargames / Rick Brennan.
      p. cm.
    "MR-1490."
    Includes bibliographical references.
    ISBN 0-8330-3153-8
      1. United States—Defenses. 2. National security—United States. 3. United
    States. Army. 4. War games. 5. Military planning—United States. I. Title.

    UA23.B7823 2002
    355.4'5'0973—dc21

                                     2002024809

Cover photos courtesy of U.S. Army and DoD Link; Cover photo credits (l-r): JTF-O; (top row) Pfc. Jeremy W. Guthrie, 314th Press Camp Headquarters, Staff Sgt. David J. Ferrier, U.S. Marine Corps, Staff Sgt. David J. Ferrier, U.S. Marine Corps; (bottom row) Staff Sgt. Steve Faulisi, U.S. Air Force

RAND is a nonprofit institution that helps improve policy and decisionmaking through research and analysis. RAND® is a registered trademark. RAND's publications do not necessarily reflect the opinions or policies of its research sponsors.

Cover design by Stephen Bloodsworth

Published 2002 by RAND
1700 Main Street, P.O. Box 2138, Santa Monica, CA 90407-2138
1200 South Hayes Street, Arlington, VA 22202-5050
201 North Craig Street, Suite 102, Pittsburgh, PA 15213
RAND URL: http://www.rand.org/
To order RAND documents or to obtain additional information, contact Distribution Services: Telephone: (310) 451-7002; Fax: (310) 451-6915; Email: order@rand.org

This paper was written before the horrific events of September 11, 2001. The Army wargames that are its focus addressed scenarios somewhat different from the terrorist attack on the Pentagon and the World Trade Center. The scenarios employed during these wargames were designed to examine more traditional forms of warfare. The attacks on the U.S. homeland differed from what was witnessed on September 11 in purpose, scale, and the amount of self-restraint exercised by the attacking force. That said, many of the insights gained from the games are relevant to current studies and analyses relating to homeland security.

As part of its study of future war, the U.S. Army's Training and Doctrine Command (TRADOC) sponsors workshops and encourages specialized games in areas of interest. Since February 1998, TRADOC has sponsored the study of homeland security as a special area of interest. RAND Arroyo Center's role in the homeland security study was to assist TRADOC by observing seminars, workshops, and wargames; reviewing seminar, workshop, and wargame briefing material; and analyzing Army doctrine and other published reports on the subject.

This report documents the Arroyo Center's analysis of the TRADOC homeland security games, seminars, and workshops since the inception of the program. The insights and issues raised here highlight new and emerging threats and vulnerabilities to the physical security of the United States. This work broadly fits into the larger body of research relating to asymmetric warfare and counterterrorism. The issues addressed will be of interest to senior military and civilian leaders with responsibilities for homeland security.

The TRADOC Deputy Chief of Staff for Doctrine sponsored this research. It was conducted in the Arroyo Center's Strategy, Doctrine, and Resources Program. The Arroyo Center is a federally funded research and development center sponsored by the United States Army.

For more information on RAND Arroyo Center, contact the Director of Operations (telephone 310-393-0411, extension 6500; FAX 310-451-6952; e-mail donnab@rand.org), or visit the Arroyo Center's Web site at http://www.rand.org/organization/ard/.

CONTENTS

SUMMARY

The Army After Next (AAN) Project and, more recently, the Army Transformation Study, Wargames, and Analysis Project have identified issues relating to homeland security. Over the course of five major wargames, a counterterrorism workshop, and a homeland security symposium, U.S. Army Training and Doctrine Command (TRADOC) has brought together senior civilian and military personnel to wrestle with hard questions about emerging threats to the United States during the period 2015 to 2020. The initial insights about homeland security emerged unexpectedly. Although the study of homeland security was not a primary area of interest for TRADOC, all wargames and workshops were partially designed to examine specific research questions relating to this topic.

This report analyzes four wargames, a counterterrorism workshop, and a homeland security symposium, all conducted between 1996 and 2000, in an effort to better understand and prepare for future warfare. At the time the games were conducted there was a lack of clarity concerning both the future threats to the homeland and the evolving role of the Army in homeland security. Indeed, within the various agencies of the U.S. government there continues to be a lack of uniformity in definitions for such terms as homeland defense, homeland security, weapons of mass destruction, crisis management, consequence management, combating terrorism, counterterrorism, and antiterrorism. While some progress has been made on these fronts, there remains a need to build a consensus within the U.S. government concerning all aspects of homeland security. Part of this consensus must include the definition of key terms associated with this mission area. Finally, such a review must explicitly state the assumed limitations imposed by U.S. law and policy, and how those differences might affect the decisionmaking process in the event of a declared war against an adversarial regime.

It is important to note that seminars and wargames are not especially well suited to developing specific organizational or operational solutions to problems. Rather, the utility of these analytical tools lies in their ability to raise issues and explore potential responses or solutions that can then be studied with more rigor. Consequently, the results of Army wargaming efforts have not produced definitive conclusions about the conduct of future warfare as it relates to protecting the homeland against asymmetric attacks. The insights gained from such activities have created fertile ground for further analysis about potential futures. While it is too early to state findings conclusively, emerging trends indicate significant vulnerabilities for the United States. As will be discussed in more detail, analysis indicates a growing potential that future adversaries will take advantage of those vulnerabilities by attacking military and civilian targets within the United States and its territories. Potential targets include critical national infrastructure, U.S. military forces, and important symbols of U.S. national power.

THREATS TO THE U.S. HOMELAND

Over the course of each wargame described in this report, Red military planners attempted to counter the overwhelming military prowess of the U.S. military by conducting limited attacks against the homeland of the United States. Recognizing that it is easier to delay, disrupt, degrade, or defeat a military force before it arrays itself for combat, all Red teams developed plans to attack the U.S. military's power-projection capabilities. Additionally, many of the Red teams attacked targets designed to undercut the willingness of the American public to engage in an overseas conflict by demonstrating their ability to inflict casualties within the U.S. homeland. The resulting insights can be grouped into seven primary categories: asymmetric warfare, direct action attacks within the United States, the concept of a self-defined "redline," counter–power projection operations, deterring U.S. military action, perception management operations, and the growing incentive for preemption by future adversaries.

Asymmetric Warfare

Broadly speaking, asymmetric warfare refers to the application of means and methods in an unanticipated and nontraditional manner; the relationship between unlike capabilities gives one side an advantage over another. In its most extreme form, asymmetric warfare causes a cascading effect out of proportion to the effort invested. Asymmetric approaches, therefore, often seek a major psychological impact to produce shock and confusion to affect the opponent's will, initiative, and freedom of action. This condition, whether it is termed disruption or disorganization, in turn creates opportunities for an inferior force to gain an advantage over a superior force. In each of the games, adversaries chose to employ asymmetric counters to the United States throughout the theater of operations. What surprised many Blue players, however, was the willingness of adversaries to challenge the United States directly in its homeland through the use of asymmetric means.

Direct Action Attacks within the United States

Each of the Red teams concluded that if conflict with the United States was inevitable, limited attacks against targets within the United States were essential to success. In an effort to gain international political support, many of the Red teams delayed the initiation of hostilities within the U.S. homeland until after the United States initiated combat operations or, in some cases, when the United States military began its deployment process. Interestingly, the threat of massive destruction by the United States did not prevent such attacks from taking place. In fact, Red teams determined that whether they attacked targets inside the borders of the United States or not, massive destruction would be inflicted upon their military forces, capabilities, and related infrastructure. Consequently, they concluded that their best chance for victory required them to keep the United States from building up forces and capabilities in the region. The goal was not just military but also political; they wanted to convince the United States that the potential costs of conflict clearly outweighed any potential gain. The only way they could achieve that goal was to attack U.S.-based targets.

The Concept of a "Redline"

While each Red team decided to conduct asymmetric attacks within the United States, they decided not to take any action that would cross what one of the teams referred to as the "redline." The redline was used to identify actions likely to trigger an unacceptable level of U.S. escalation and elicit a determined American response to achieve a "total victory." In fact, Red teams were careful to select the targets and weapons that would achieve the greatest military and political impact without doing something that would give the U.S. government the moral justification to seek the total destruction of the adversary. Based upon this self-imposed limitation, Red team participants decided to attack the United States hard enough to delay the arrival of U.S. forces in theater, but not so hard as to cause a "Pearl Harbor effect."

For similar reasons, Red teams shied away from using large-scale "terrorist" attacks against civilian targets, instead electing to primarily use "direct action" attacks against important military and infrastructure targets. This decision was made because team members concluded that unlike terrorist organizations, which are difficult to target and destroy, a nation-state that is responsible for killing hundreds or thousands of civilians would quickly find itself facing the full fury of the U.S. government. It is also important to note that many of the Red teams concluded that "limited use" of certain chemical and biological agents against military targets probably would not cross the American "redline," although it might if the casualty count became too high. Whether this assessment is correct is less important than the fact that Red team participants believed it was correct. This raises the question of whether future adversaries will come to the same conclusion.

Counter–Power Projection Operations

Recognizing that it is easier to delay, disrupt, degrade, or defeat a military force before it arrays itself for combat, all Red teams developed plans to attack U.S. military power-projection capabilities in the United States. The advantage of this operational concept was articulated by General Giulio Douhet in 1921, when he stated that "it is easier and more effective to destroy the enemy's aerial power by destroying his nests and eggs on the ground than to hunt his flying birds in the air." During game play, each Red team concluded that if conflict with the United States was inevitable, limited attacks within its homeland were essential to victory.

Deterring U.S. Military Action

A future adversary that acquires the capability to attack civilian and military targets within the United States using asymmetric means has the potential to threaten attacks as a response to U.S. deployment. During the 1997 Summer Wargame, which portrayed a conflict in which U.S. vital interests were not directly threatened, Blue political leadership delayed the deployment of initial entry special operations forces until after the perceived threat to the U.S. homeland had been largely eliminated. While the delay only lasted for a few weeks, it poses an interesting question: if a much smaller military adversary gains a credible capability to threaten serious damage inside the U.S. homeland, will it be able to deter U.S. military action?

Perception Management Operations

The key to a successful campaign against the United States may be a well-developed perception management effort. Indeed, Red team participants noted, without exception, that a carefully executed perception management campaign was a critically important component of their strategy to defeat the United States. Perception management can be effectively used to shape how a population and relevant political support groups view given aspects of an operation. The effective use of modern communications and media technologies may enable other governments, factions, and splinter groups to counter U.S. military superiority in the theater of operations by targeting U.S. and coalition populations with symbolic images, events, and propaganda designed to undercut support for the operation. Further, potential competitors may use disinformation, propaganda, and agitation to destroy U.S. and coalition legitimacy. The U.S. government is at an inherent disadvantage when countering perception management operations, especially in parts of the world such as the Middle East, Asia, and Latin America where U.S. motivations are held suspect by an overwhelmingly large portion of the population.

Incentives for Preemptive Attacks

One of the most striking observations to come from the wargames is the magnitude of the incentive that potential adversaries have to conduct preemptive attacks against the United States. Given America's overwhelming conventional power-projection capabilities, future adversaries cannot afford to permit the United States to mobilize and deploy forces to theater. Therefore, each of the Red teams carefully examined the utility of attacking certain critical nodes before the onset of hostilities. In an effort to minimize the scale of U.S. intervention, this approach was rarely taken, and even when it was adopted, attacks were limited and covert. Targets for preemptive action included logistics infrastructure, command and control sites, space assets, select airfields, ammunition storage sites, seaports, and airports. While this concept is not altogether new, the discussion by Red planning staffs highlighted the fact that a future opponent, by attacking a relatively small number of carefully chosen targets, could significantly degrade U.S. warfighting capabilities. In addition, the Red teams concluded that by striking multiple high-value targets they could establish a credible threat of future, large-scale escalation.

EMERGING ISSUES

The following issues were raised during "national policy team" deliberations by wargame participants who were role-playing senior government officials such as the President, Secretary of State, Secretary of Defense, Attorney General, and so forth. While sufficient analysis was not conducted during the wargames to develop findings or conclusions, these issues were the subject of debate and require further study.

- Paramilitary or covert attacks within the United States may have the potential to blur the line between law enforcement and military operations. For instance, an attack on U.S. critical infrastructure or command and control sites such as the Pentagon could be considered either an act of terrorism or an act of war. At what point does a hostile act cross the line from a crime to a national security threat? What new organizational structures, policies, and procedures are required to integrate the capabilities of the U.S. government to defend against and respond to attacks on the homeland?

- Attacks against U.S. critical infrastructure, military command and control structure, and critical deployment sites could significantly degrade the deployment process of the U.S. military. This is, however, little more than an assertion that has not yet been quantified. To what extent could the deployment of U.S. forces be disrupted by relatively small attacks within the homeland? How might the effects of these attacks be mitigated?

- If such attacks are probable, DoD must reassess the current practice of consolidating military bases, power-projection facilities, ammunition depots, and other sites necessary to prosecute a war overseas. While consolidation may enable greater efficiencies during peace, it may also exacerbate vulnerabilities during times of conflict. For instance, during times of conflict large bases and depots are likely to be viewed as high-value targets by potential adversaries because the loss of any one of them could significantly affect the U.S. response. This negative aspect of consolidation should be addressed in any future BRAC discussion. To what extent does base consolidation increase exacerbate vulnerabilities during conflict? How might the United States gain the efficiencies associated with consolidation while minimizing potential vulnerabilities?

- It is important to assess the actual and potential competition for military resources—personnel, units, and equipment—that is likely to occur if the United States is facing attacks on its homeland while prosecuting a war overseas. To what extent could this competition for resources hinder the ability of the United States to prosecute the war? What options might mitigate the effect of this competition for resources—especially for high-demand/low-density personnel and units?

- It is necessary to examine how DoD and the nation are organized to meet this emerging threat. Both U.S. law and the American way of life mandate a strong civilian presence within the homeland security framework. Under what conditions would the military be asked to take a more direct and prominent role in homeland security? What are the training and doctrine implications of this potentiality?

- Existing statutes may not adequately anticipate asymmetric military attacks in the homeland and, consequently, create a perceived legal barrier that is likely to impede the initial response of the military. Do existing statutes provide sufficient legal basis and clarity to prepare for future asymmetric attacks within the United States? If not, what specific legislation would provide the necessary statutory authority to counter such threats?

The questions raised by the foregoing analysis are: How should America's Army be prepared to help defend the American homeland? Which organizations should be funded, manned, trained, equipped, and organized to confront this threat? Can local, state, or federal law enforcement be expected to counter a military or paramilitary threat—albeit a threat with relatively limited capabilities? If this is a mission for the Army, are the selected units enabled by appropriate organizations, doctrine, training, and equipment to meet the threat—given legal constraints such as Posse Comitatus that are designed to limit military operations within the homeland? How might the Army work in conjunction with law enforcement in such situations?

HOMELAND SECURITY AND THE ARMY'S TRANSFORMATION

From a gaming perspective, TRADOC must determine a way to examine homeland security and simultaneously explore new operational and organizational concepts associated with future war overseas. If the 1998 Spring Wargame is any indication, homeland security has the potential to dominate game play. While this may most closely approximate reality, it is also important to examine other key goals of the Army Transformation process. Developing a parallel process for examining issues associated with homeland security can help solve this problem. Such an effort might include the establishment of an annual workshop and the inclusion of a homeland security team in the annual Army Transformation Wargame. A second option would be the establishment of a separate homeland security game designed to stress the Army's future Objective Force by conducting homeland security operations while also conducting an overseas operation against a major opponent.

CONCLUSIONS

Homeland security is not the exclusive responsibility of law enforcement or the Defense Department; it is the responsibility of both—working together with numerous other federal, state, and local agencies. Because homeland security falls between institutional lines of authority, it is an issue that, unfortunately, may not be examined until *after* an event occurs that conclusively proves there is a requirement for change. The United States has a long history of waiting for an event to occur before taking actions that could prevent disasters. One need only think about Beirut, Khobar Towers, Mogadishu, USS *Cole,* and September 11 to understand the effect of asymmetric attacks. All of these might have been prevented had we been better prepared. In each case, signs and warnings were available but were not acted upon.

As discussed earlier, a growing body of literature suggests that future adversaries are likely to employ asymmetric attacks within the United States to deter, degrade, disrupt, delay, and/or destroy U.S. forces before they can arrive in theater. If successful, these attacks could cause the United States serious problems in the next military conflict or other military operation. If only partially successful, such attacks would still significantly complicate the deployment process and also probably result in the loss of American military and civilian lives.

Stewardship requires the Army to examine its potential roles and missions in all facets of homeland security—from preventing attacks to helping civil authorities respond to the consequences of such attacks. Although the Army is more comfortable with the latter, it cannot and should not avoid the former.

ACKNOWLEDGMENTS

The author gratefully acknowledges the assistance of LTC Monroe Nickell, U.S. Army Maneuver Support Center, for ensuring that appropriate game data were made available. I would also like to thank Mr. Larry Heystek of the U.S. Army Training and Doctrine Command and LTC Antulio J. Echevarria II from the U.S. Army War College for sharing their thoughts and ideas about the Army's role in homeland security. The insights and issues addressed in this report belong to the author, but our discussions helped to focus and refine the concepts contained herein.

ABBREVIATIONS

AAN	Army After Next
ABL	Airborne Laser
AC	Active Component
AT	Antiterrorism
APOD	Aerial Port of Debarkation
APOE	Aerial Port of Embarkation
ATWG	Army Transformation Wargame
BF	Battle Force
CNA	Computer Network Attack
CBRN	Chemical, Biological, Radiological, and Nuclear
CIA	Central Intelligence Agency
CINC	Commander in Chief
CJCS	Chairman, Joint Chiefs of Staff
CND	Computer Network Defense
CONUS	Continental United States
CSA	Chief of Staff, U.S. Army
CT	Counterterrorism
DCSDOC	Deputy Chief of Staff for Doctrine (TRADOC)
DoD	Department of Defense

DIA	Defense Intelligence Agency
DOJ	Department of Justice
FBI	Federal Bureau of Investigation
FEMA	Federal Emergency Management Agency
HLS	Homeland Security
IO	Information Operations
ISR	Intelligence Surveillance and Reconnaissance
JSOC	Joint Special Operations Command
LEA	Law Enforcement Agencies
MTW	Major Theater War
NCA	National Command Authority
NIR	New Independent Republic
NNM	New Nationalist Movement
NSA	National Security Agency
RC	Reserve Component
RMA	Revolution in Military Affairs
SAM	Surface-to-Air Missile
SOF	Special Operations Forces
SPOD	Seaport of Debarkation
SPOE	Seaport of Embarkation
STO	Special Technical Operations
SWG	Spring Wargame
TRADOC	U.S. Army Training and Doctrine Command
USAF	United States Air Force
USMC	United States Marine Corps
WMD	Weapons of Mass Destruction
WWG	Winter Wargame

Chapter One

INTRODUCTION

The Army After Next (AAN) Project and, more recently, the Army Transformation Study, Wargames, and Analysis Project have identified a number of issues relating to homeland security while focusing on the conduct of future warfare.[1] Over the course of five major wargames, a counterterrorism workshop, and a homeland security symposium, U.S. Army Training and Doctrine Command (TRADOC) has brought together senior civilian and military personnel to wrestle with hard questions about emerging threats to the United States and its territories during times of conflict.[2] Indeed, insights gained from the first two AAN wargames conducted in 1996 created the underpinnings for subsequent analyses of asymmetric warfare conducted by both the Office of the Secretary of Defense and the Joint Staff.[3] Initial insights about homeland security emerged unexpectedly.

---

[1]The Army After Next Project was initiated in 1996 and continued until the summer of 1999. Beginning in 1999 the U.S. Army Training and Doctrine Command established the Army Transformation Study, Wargames, and Analysis Project. While the first project was designed to develop future operational and organizational concepts, the charter of the current project is more focused on transforming the Army by fielding the Objective Force in the 2010 time frame.

[2]Most military participants held the rank of lieutenant colonel or higher. Similarly, most civilian government participants generally held the grade of GS-14 or GS-15, although a number of former ambassadors and senior executives also participated.

[3]The most exhaustive examination of asymmetric warfare as it relates to future military operations was conducted by the Joint Staff (J5/Strategy) and culminated with the publication of the *Joint Strategic Review, 1999 (JSR-99)*. In addition, as part of its ongoing Power Projection Net Assessment, the Office of the Secretary of Defense (Net Assessment) has recently focused a significant amount of effort on examining asymmetric warfare. A significant part of the study was devoted to homeland security issues.

Although the study of homeland security was not a primary area of interest for TRADOC, parts of later wargames and workshops were designed to examine specific research questions relating to this topic. Since 1998, however, the analysis of issues associated with homeland security has been conducted virtually separate from the larger study about future war.

It is important to note that seminars and wargames are not especially well suited to the task of developing specific organizational or operational solutions to problems. Rather, the utility of these analytical tools lies in their ability to raise issues and explore potential responses or solutions that can then be studied with more rigor. Consequently, Army wargaming efforts have not produced definitive conclusions about the conduct of future warfare as it relates to protecting the homeland against asymmetric attacks. The insights gained from such activities, however, have created fertile ground for further analysis about potential futures. While it is too early to state conclusive findings, emerging trends indicate vulnerabilities for the United States. As will be discussed in more detail, analysis indicates a growing potential for future adversaries to take advantage of those vulnerabilities by attacking military and civilian targets within the United States and its territories. Potential targets include critical national infrastructure, U.S. military forces, and important symbols of U.S. national power.

SETTING THE STAGE

The Army After Next Project was established in 1996 by the Chief of Staff of the Army (CSA) to help create a vision for future requirements and establish a linkage between Force XXI and the long-range vision. As stated in 1996, the mission of AAN is to "[c]onduct broad studies of warfare to about the year 2020 to frame issues vital to the development of the U.S. Army after about 2010, and to provide those issues to the senior Army Leadership in a format suitable for integration into TRADOC development (R&D) programs."[4] Consequently, the project's dominant focus is the development of operational and organizational concepts that enable the Army to deploy rapidly to

---

[4]Headquarters, U.S. Army Training and Doctrine Command, *Army After Next Project: Report to the Chief of Staff of the Army*, June 1996, p. 2.

distant theaters, to prevail in combat against a wide spectrum of opponents, and to achieve rapid victory for the United States.

To accomplish these goals, it was assumed that the majority of future Army forces would begin the deployment process from forts and bases located within the United States. A smaller number of forces would remain forward deployed and would be available for redeployment in times of crisis. Moreover, future Army forces were credited with tactical and operational dominance in all aspects of game play. This assumed battlefield dominance of an Army dependent upon power projection caused Red (i.e., opposing) team leaders to plan for the use of special operations forces and covert agents to disrupt, degrade, and delay the deployment of U.S. forces. As early as 1996, the AAN hypothesized that a potential adversary might choose to "expand hostilities as rapidly as possible outside his region and even into the U.S. homeland in an effort to defeat the overwhelming battlefield capabilities of the United States."[5] Interestingly, in every wargame the Red military staff contemplated military strikes within the United States both to prevent the successful employment of U.S. forces overseas and to establish some form of strategic symmetry in which homeland risks were not just limited to Red. Thus, from the standpoint of the Red commanders, the question was not whether to attack forces inside the United States, but when and how to conduct such attacks.

This report analyzes four wargames, a counterterrorism workshop, and a homeland security symposium, all conducted between 1996 and 2000 in an effort to better understand and prepare for future warfare. At the time the games were conducted there was a lack of clarity on both the future threats to the homeland and the evolving role of the Army in homeland security. Indeed, within the various agencies of the U.S. government there is still no uniformity in definitions for such terms as homeland defense, homeland security, weapons of mass destruction, crisis management, consequence management, combating terrorism, counterterrorism, and antiterrorism. While some progress has been made on all these fronts, there remains a need to build a consensus within the U.S. government concerning all aspects of homeland security. Part of this

---

[5]*Army After Next Project: Report to the Chief of Staff of the Army*, June 1996, pp. 10–11.

consensus must include definitions of key terms associated with this mission area. Finally, work must be done to explicitly state the assumed limitations imposed by U.S. law and policy, and how those limitations might affect the decisionmaking process in the event of a declared war against an adversarial regime.

PURPOSE

The purpose of this report is to highlight insights and issues regarding homeland security generated by TRADOC's Army After Next and Army Transformation Study, Wargames, and Analysis projects and to make recommendations concerning future research and analysis.

ORGANIZATION OF THIS REPORT

Chapter Two provides an overview of the organization and execution of TRADOC-sponsored wargames and workshops as they relate to homeland security. Chapter Three addresses key insights about homeland security derived from the games. Chapter Four identifies issues that require further analysis. Finally, Chapter Five provides recommendations on ways to better incorporate homeland security into the Army Transformation Wargame process.

Chapter Two

HISTORY OF HOMELAND SECURITY IN ARMY WARGAMING

The methodology used by the Army After Next Project and, more recently, the Army Transformation Study, Wargames, and Analysis Project to examine homeland security is an evolving one.[1] During the 1997 Winter Wargame, the game structure and organization did not directly address homeland security. Moreover, no substantial analysis was conducted to assess the potential military response to an attack within the United States against purely civilian targets such as the World Trade Center, so the topic was not part of the wargame series. Currently, homeland security issues are examined by TRADOC primarily as a "franchise" event conducted under the auspices of the U.S. Army Maneuver Support Center at Fort Leonard Wood, Missouri. This chapter provides an overview of the organization and execution of key TRADOC homeland security activities.

WINTER WARGAME, 1997

The first Army After Next wargame was conducted in the winter of 1997. This game focused on designing a future force and developing appropriate operational concepts for the 2025 time period.[2] The adversary chosen for this wargame possessed not only nuclear

---

[1]During the early phases of the AAN project, the term homeland defense was used to discuss military counterterrorism and "counter-SOF" operations conducted within the United States. Since 1999, the term homeland security has gained greater acceptance within the Army.

[2]The title Winter Wargame was selected to differentiate this operational/strategic wargame from a number of smaller preparatory tactical wargames that were conducted in the winter of 1996 and the spring of 1997.

weapons, but also a large, powerful, and fully modernized conventional military force. This "near-peer" competitor was designed to challenge the full spectrum of U.S. military capabilities.

Homeland security was not specifically played during this first wargame. Nevertheless, a significant discussion took place in the Red planning cell about the value of preemptive attacks on U.S. forces to preclude their timely arrival in theater. While a number of military plans for attacking the United States were developed, the Red political leaders were reluctant to authorize an attack on the U.S. homeland, convinced that such actions would cause them to lose political and diplomatic support in the international community. Moreover, the Red political leadership was not willing to attack the homeland of the United States because of the possibility of creating a "Pearl Harbor effect"—energizing the will of the American public and alienating the international community. Not only was Red reluctant to conduct physical attacks against military targets located within the United States, it was also unwilling to employ information operations against U.S. space-related ground facilities, believing that such attacks violated the "homeland sanctuary" of the United States.[3]

Throughout the wargame, however, the Red military commander continued to request authorization for selective attacks on militarily significant targets within the United States. Toward the end of the game, after the U.S. military attacked targets inside the adversary's homeland, the Red political leadership authorized special operations forces and covert action agents to conduct attacks inside the United States. These attacks came too late to influence the outcome of the war. Moreover, even when the United States was attacked, the game controllers made decisions that caused the attack to have very little effect on the outcome of the wargame.

Although a number of unexpected insights were generated from the 1997 Winter Wargame, no mention was made of the potential threats to the United States in any of the reports. Homeland defense was not addressed in TRADOC's annual report on the Army After Next Project to the Chief of Staff of the Army, but many Red team participants

_____

[3]Walter L. Perry and Marc Dean Millot, *Issues from the 1997 Army After Next Winter Wargame*, Santa Monica, CA: RAND, MR-988-A, 1998, p. 23.

walked away from the event questioning the underlying assumption that the United States would remain a sanctuary in the 2020 period.[4]

DOMESTIC COUNTERTERRORISM WORKSHOP

Following the Winter Wargame, TRADOC was approached by one of the Red team members and asked to consider the impact of a militarily significant attack, conducted within the United States, on early-deploying forces. To examine this issue, TRADOC decided to conduct an interagency workshop on domestic counterterrorism that would include a cross-section of federal agencies. In total, the workshop consisted of twenty-two people representing nine federal agencies.[5]

During the April 1997 workshop, participants struggled over the definition of the problem. Some argued that attacks within the United States were not necessarily terrorism,[6] but could be conceived of as acts of asymmetric warfare. Workshop participants also examined the changing character of terrorism, the distinction between terrorism and asymmetric warfare, and potential U.S. vulnerabilities both today and in the future.[7]

---

[4]U.S. Army Training and Doctrine Command, *Army After Next Project: Report to the Chief of Staff of the Army, Knowledge & Speed*, 1997.

[5]The following agencies and offices were represented in the workshop: Department of State, Federal Bureau of Investigation, Department of Transportation, Federal Emergency Management Agency, National Security Agency, Central Intelligence Agency, Department of Health and Human Services, Department of Energy, and the Department of Defense.

[6]For the purposes of this report, terrorism is defined as acts of violence, or threatened acts of violence, used to create an atmosphere of fear and alarm designed to coerce others into actions they otherwise would not undertake, or into refraining from actions that they desire to take. All terrorist acts committed within the United States are crimes in violation of federal law (Title 18, U.S. Code). Further, this violence or threat of violence is generally directed against civilian targets, and is conducted in such a way as to gain maximum publicity. Finally, terrorist acts are designed to produce effects far beyond the immediate physical damage they cause. For a more thorough definition of terrorism, see Karen Gardela and Bruce Hoffman, *The RAND Chronology of International Terrorism for 1986*, Santa Monica, CA: RAND, R-3890-RC, 1990, p. 1.

[7]Army After Next 1997 Summer Wargame, *Domestic Counterterrorism Workshop Briefing Book*, Science Applications International Corporation, June 1997.

Although a consensus on many issues was elusive, most participants believed that the best defense against attacks on the United States was a comprehensive intelligence program and specially designated military and law enforcement units trained to preempt or respond to these incidents. The requirement for DoD assistance within the United States would be especially acute if a future adversary chose to conduct multiple, nearly simultaneous attacks against militarily significant or symbolic targets within the United States. Many participants argued that this type of attack would overwhelm federal, state, and local law enforcement agencies, as well as other first responders, and could delay the deployment of U.S. military forces during times of conflict.

SUMMER WARGAME, 1997

The 1997 Summer Wargame was designed to test the ability of Blue (i.e., U.S.) forces to assist a friendly government in defeating an insurgency that was closely associated with an international criminal cartel. The Green team played the friendly government, while the Orange team played the insurgency—the New Nationalist Movement (NNM). As part of game control, TRADOC established a Domestic Counter-Terrorism (DCT) cell for the wargame. This cell provided subject matter expertise to help both Blue and Orange develop reasonable plans that would facilitate a better understanding of the military implications of terrorist attacks in the United States during times of conflict, especially when less-than-vital interests are at stake.[8]

Given the overwhelming combat superiority of the Blue forces, the Orange political leadership sought to develop plans that would deter Blue's involvement and, if deterrence failed, would delay or degrade the arrival of Blue forces in theater. Within the United States, Orange agents infiltrated student organizations, established public relations offices, and created a number of front companies both to manage their "business operations" and to serve as handlers for covert agents.

---

[8]Army After Next 1997 Summer Wargame, *Domestic Counterterrorism Team Notebook*, Doctrine Directorate, TRADOC, September 1997, p. 2.

When it became clear that conflict was inevitable, Blue forces began to take initial steps toward deploying forces to assist Green. However, Orange took an unusual step and leaked information about its capability and willingness to conduct multiple large-scale terrorist operations within the United States if the United States entered the conflict.[9] This disclosure prompted the Blue President to authorize the employment of all National Technical Means to assist the FBI to "locate and apprehend" suspected Orange covert agents.[10]

Because vital U.S. interests were not at stake, the Blue President further decided to delay the deployment of U.S. forces until he was convinced that the majority of Orange agents had either been captured or their whereabouts identified. This was a contentious issue because many of the Blue players believed that the United States should not "give in to terrorism." Nevertheless, the Blue President argued that he was unwilling to place American citizens at risk simply to facilitate a rapid deployment of military forces in a conflict where less-than-vital interests were at stake. Finally, over the strong objection of the Chairman of the Joint Chiefs of Staff (CJCS), the Blue President decided to delay the deployment of special mission units that are typically under the control of the Joint Special Operations Command (JSOC) in the event that the FBI or other law enforcement agencies needed assistance.

During the Senior Leader Seminar, the Blue President stated that asymmetric responses can create explicit linkages among domestic security, international security, and general policy concerns which, together, will limit options for policymakers.[11] In this game, asymmetries directed against citizens within the United States had a crippling effect on the willingness of the Blue political leadership to enter a conflict until the large-scale terrorist threat was eliminated.

---

[9]For game play purposes, it was estimated that Orange had several hundred agents within the United States.

[10]Questions were raised about the authority to use National Technical Means and whether such information could be used in court, given constitutional as well as national security constraints. The Blue President decided to pursue court orders whenever possible, but he emphasized that the conviction of enemy agents was less important than the protection of American lives and property.

[11]Army After Next 1997 Summer Wargame, *Senior Leader Seminar Briefing Book*, TRADOC, 18 September 1997.

SPRING WARGAME, 1998

The 1998 Spring Wargame consisted of 2 two-sided wargames where Red and Orange forces simultaneously challenged Blue forces.[12] Orange represented the New Nationalist Movement, which was threatening a friendly government in Asia. The Red forces in this game represented the New Independent Republic (NIR), which was the dominant political, economic, and military power in the Persian Gulf region. In addition to a modernized military capable of rapidly invading neighboring countries, the NIR had a nuclear capability, ballistic missile delivery systems, and stockpiles of both chemical and biological weapons.

The Red political and military leadership concluded that it could achieve victory only if it could move rapidly enough to occupy key portions of Saudi Arabia before the United States could respond either politically or militarily to the crisis. To freeze Blue politically, Red waged an extensive propaganda campaign designed to convince the U.S. public and international community that Red only sought to "liberate" holy cities in Saudi Arabia to allow unencumbered access to all Muslims—including Americans. When Blue forces began air and missile attacks against NIR forces, the Red military commander "reluctantly" initiated limited attacks against CONUS military airfields and selected ports of embarkation to delay and degrade the arrival of Blue forces in theater.[13] It is also important to note that the NIR attacks in the United States were timed to assure that they could be justified as legitimate reciprocity for Blue attacks on the Red homeland.

The Red threat to CONUS-based facilities posed in this game was substantial. For planning purposes, Blue was informed that there were between 500 and 700 enemy special operations personnel and covert agents within the United States. Moreover, given their level of training, it was determined that Red special operations forces (SOF) had the potential to conduct a coordinated attack at multiple locations within the United States. Additionally, the Blue policy team

---

[12]Army After Next 1998 Spring Wargame, *Reference Book Volume I and II*, TRADOC, April 1998.

[13]Army After Next 1998 Spring Wargame, *Senior Leader Seminar Briefing Book*, TRADOC, 30 April 1998.

was told that the primary focus of Red SOF was most likely to be militarily significant targets associated with the deployment of U.S. forces and capabilities. Finally, while it was recognized that chemical or biological agents might be used, Blue reasoned that weapons of mass destruction (WMD) would only be used as a last resort—if the survival of the Red regime were threatened.

Given this scenario, the Blue President decided to create a Task Force led by the Deputy Attorney General—a position created by the Blue team specifically to address this issue. The Task Force membership included the Department of Justice, Department of Defense, Department of Customs, Department of Treasury, and the Federal Emergency Management Agency. Additionally, intelligence support was provided by a number of agencies, including the Central Intelligence Agency (CIA), Defense Intelligence Agency (DIA), and National Security Agency (NSA).[14] Further, the military commander in chief (CINC) responsible for CONUS-based forces was directed to create three Joint Task Forces (JTFs) to provide command and control for military forces operating within the United States. One of these JTFs, JTF Crisis Response, was also designated as the Joint Special Operations Command (JSOC). The JSOC commander remained under the command of the CINC and controlled all military forces assigned crisis response missions, including national mission units that have counterterrorism responsibilities. Consistent with an Operation Order approved by the National Command Authority (NCA), the JSOC commander received taskings for operations conducted within the United States directly from the Deputy Attorney General.[15]

The organization chart depicted in Figure 1 reflects the organization discussed during the wargame. The principal concept underlying this structure was that the Deputy Attorney General would have "tasking authority" for all national elements that had a responsibility for homeland defense. With respect to DoD assets, JTFs were placed

---

[14]This list of agencies and departments is not all-inclusive. Rather, it is illustrative of the desire of game participants to provide the Deputy Attorney General, in his role as Coordinator for Homeland Defense, with budgetary and tasking authority for all national assets that could be brought to bear on this problem.

[15]The Deputy Attorney General was given Cabinet-level status and was a viewed as a principal on the National Security Council for matters relating to homeland defense.

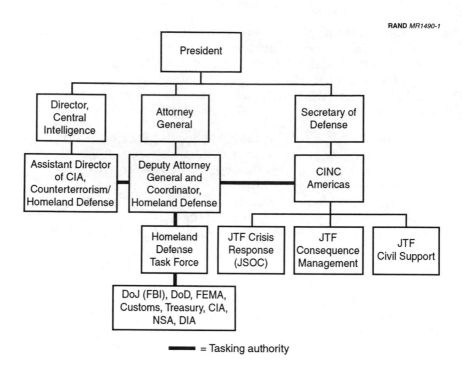

RAND *MR1490-1*

Figure 1—Homeland Defense Task Force Organization

under the operational control of the Attorney General, but remained under the command of the Secretary of Defense/CINC.

Within the construct, CINC Americas is a force provider for all warfighting CINCs. Thus, it was anticipated that conflicts could and would arise between competing requirements. As in all other cases where there is a competition for resources among CINCs, the NCA would determine which theater would receive the priority of support. In essence, the Blue policy team considered the Deputy Attorney General in the same light as a warfighting CINC. The difference was that he was responsible for fighting and winning the war on the American front.

While no one considered this organization "the answer" to the problem, it was an attempt to balance the statutory requirements of command and control of military forces with the need to provide personnel and capabilities to the individual who had been given the responsibility for homeland defense.[16]

SPRING WARGAME, 1999

Early in the planning stages for the 1999 Spring Wargame, it was decided that the homeland security aspect would be downplayed so that it didn't detract from the game's primary research objective: developing insights on a hybrid Army in the 2020 period.[17] So even though the adversary placed a high priority on attacking the U.S. homeland, the game did not consider the impact of these attacks. For example, early in the operation Red employed information operations to target Blue communications and data systems, transportation infrastructure, stock exchange, and military deployment systems. Later in the operation, Red attacked the Blue homeland using space-based lasers (SBL) and weapons of mass destruction. Although these attacks were not adjudicated by the game controllers, they did prompt a lengthy debate within the Blue policy team on how to respond to the homeland security challenge.

Unlike previous TRADOC games, no effort was made to assess what impact these types of attacks would have on U.S. power-projection capabilities. While this wargame reaffirmed the fact that the United States could be vulnerable to a wide range of threats when confronting a determined adversary, it failed to address any of these issues seriously during subsequent postgame written analysis.

---

[16]This is not the type of relationship that exists today. According to current practice, U.S. military forces operating within the United States would remain under the control of the National Command Authority. Consequently, taskings for all activities would have to come from the Secretary of Defense and through the Chairman of the Joint Chiefs of Staff. The players understood this relationship; however, they saw no reason to conclude that operational control for missions already agreed upon could not be exercised by a senior civilian official outside of the Department of Defense. Indeed, foreign commanders within both the context of NATO and the United Nations have exercised operational control of U.S. forces. The players argued that if a foreign military officer could exercise operational control over U.S. military forces, then the Deputy Attorney General could as well.

[17]For the purpose of this game, the term "hybrid" was used to portray an Army with a mix of current forces armed with upgraded versions of today's weapon systems, Strike Forces, and Battle Forces.

HOMELAND SECURITY SPRING SYMPOSIUM, 2000

Following the 1999 Spring Wargame, responsibility for examining homeland security was delegated to the United States Army Maneuver Support Center (MANSCEN) at Fort Leonard Wood, Missouri. Rather than conducting a wargame, the MANSCEN held a homeland security symposium on March 14–16, 2000. Its intent was to bring together major Army organizations involved in homeland security and civil support operations. The key question discussed during the symposium was, "[w]hat is the role of the Army in homeland security, especially in light of the potential use of Weapons of Mass Destruction."[18] The primary goal of the symposium was to "provide a frank and open discussion between players" concerning the establishment of a TRADOC Program Integration Office for homeland security at Fort Leonard Wood. Each of the schools located at Fort Leonard Wood (Chemical, Military Police, and Engineer) provided participants and "analyzed their own capability to respond to a WMD attack using existing force structure, equipment, doctrine, and training." Concluding that there were no "universal Doctrine or Training standards for homeland security missions," the symposium participants decided that there is a need for either a Program Integration Office or Center of Excellence for homeland security.[19]

This symposium marked a major shift in the focus of homeland security efforts sponsored by TRADOC. Rather than examining potential new roles and missions that the Army might have to perform because of enemy attacks against militarily significant targets during times of future conflict, the symposium focused on what the Army can and should do today. Not surprisingly, this near-term institutional focus resulted in discussions of crisis-response and consequence-management activities undertaken to support civil authorities as a result of a WMD attack by terrorists.

---

[18]Memorandum from the Homeland Security Office (MANSCEN) to the Commander, USA Training and Doctrine Command, Subject: Homeland Security Army After Next Game Results, dated 27 July 2000.

[19]Ibid.

Chapter Three

INSIGHTS AND ISSUES

The Army After Next and Army Transformation Study, Wargames, and Analysis projects have produced a rich set of insights and issues about homeland security that can be used as the basis for further development. The lessons learned from the game series can be separated into three types.

- Defining homeland security

- Key insights on emerging threats in the United States

- Emerging issues for further analysis

While it is too early to state conclusions, emerging trends indicate vulnerabilities within the United States when its military is attempting to conduct combat operations overseas. Analysis suggests a growing probability that future adversaries may take advantage of those vulnerabilities by attacking targets within the United States in an effort to deter, degrade, disrupt, delay, or destroy U.S. military forces before they can arrive in theater.[1] The following insights and

---

[1]In addition to insights and postgame analysis derived from these TRADOC-sponsored games, other DoD-sponsored studies have reached similar conclusions. A more detailed description of the emerging threat can be found in a number of reports. *Assessment of the Impact of Chemical and Biological Weapons on Joint Operations at Aerial Ports of Embarkation in 2010*, Booz-Allen & Hamilton, October 1998, is also known as the "Pope/Bragg Study." It was a follow-on effort to the "CB 2010 Study," in which a panel of retired general officers with expertise in power-projection operations assessed the impact of chemical and biological weapons on joint operations in the 2010 time frame. See also *Assessment of the Impact of Chemical and Biological Weapons on Joint Operations in 2010: A Summary Report*, also known as the "CB 2010 Study," Booz-Allen & Hamilton, November 1997. While the Summary Report is

issues provide an initial assessment about a potential fault line between national defense and law enforcement.

DEFINING HOMELAND SECURITY

During most of the Cold War, the existing security environment insulated the United States from direct military attacks on its homeland through a complex linkage between conventional escalation and nuclear deterrence. Given these conditions, the Army was free to focus on overseas military threats, leaving the limited domestic security concerns in the capable hands of law enforcement. Given a potential conflict with another major power in the future, many of the constraints imposed by the Cold War would likely reappear. However, as evidenced by the attacks on September 11, the United States can no longer be considered a sanctuary—either from terrorist attacks, attacks against critical infrastructure, or state-directed enemy special operations attacks. While such attacks could occur at any time, they would pose especially difficult problems when conducted in support of a large-scale enemy operation conducted overseas.

During the course of the Army After Next Project, and then in the Army Transformation Study, Wargames, and Analysis Project, the definition of the problem has changed from counterterrorism to "homeland defense" and is now described as "homeland security." The evolution of this label reflects a deeper understanding of the challenges that the United States is likely to confront. What exactly does homeland security entail? Under what authority will military units operate? While many definitions of this term have been offered, none have been fully endorsed by the national security establishment. In this case, the definition of the subject has important implications for potential mission areas, tasks to be performed, and specific responsibilities.

---

unclassified with limited distribution, the full report is not available to the general public. Finally, a more detailed description of how specific adversaries might conduct such attacks is contained in the Joint Strategic Review for 1999 (JSR99) and its supporting briefings prepared by the intelligence community, *Joint Strategic Review 1999*, Washington, D.C.: The Joint Staff.

Over the last several months the Army has been wrestling with these issues in an attempt to develop an agreed-upon definition for homeland security. Before the September 11 attacks on the World Trade Center and the Pentagon, the Army defined homeland security as

> those active and passive measures taken to protect the population, area, and infrastructure of the United States, its possessions, and territories by: deterring, defending against, and mitigating the effects of threats, disasters, and attacks; supporting civil authorities in crisis and consequence management; and, helping to ensure the availability, integrity, survivability, and adequacy of critical national assets.[2]

This definition encompasses both civilian and military tasks associated with all aspects of homeland security, including detection, prevention, and response. Consequently, it establishes the framework for a national definition that can be used to highlight the importance of building a national, integrated response to the challenge.

Since the September 11 attacks, however, the definition of homeland security has been revised to include "the prevention, preemption, and deterrence of, and defense against aggression targeted at U.S. territory, sovereignty, domestic population, and infrastructure, as well as the management of the consequences of such aggression; and other domestic civil support."[3] As Secretary of the Army Thomas White stated to Congress, this construct of homeland security "includes two simultaneous and mutually supporting functions": homeland defense and civil support.[4] Homeland defense includes the protection of U.S. territory, domestic population, and critical infrastructure against military or foreign terrorist attacks; civil support involves all DoD support to civil authorities for natural and manmade domestic emergencies, civil disturbances, and designated law enforcement efforts.

---

[2]This definition is contained in *Army Homeland Security (HLS) Strategic Planning Guidance: Coordinating Draft*, Office of the Deputy Chief of Staff for Operations, Headquarters, Department of the Army, September 10, 2001.

[3]The Honorable Thomas E. White, Secretary of the Army, Statement provided to the Committee on Armed Services, United States Senate, October 25, 2001.

[4]Ibid.

It is incorrect to assume that an act of terrorism inside the United States, for which the FBI and FEMA each has significant responsibilities, necessarily means that DoD, and hence the Army, will have only an inconsequential role. Nor does it follow that the military will be called upon only when civil capabilities are overwhelmed. As it applies to terrorist attacks inside the United States, any definition must be broad enough to include all potential military activities to support civil authorities for either prevention or response, "crisis" or "consequence" management. The current definition appears robust enough to encompass all possible missions the Army may be assigned within the borders of the United States.

Whether the task is labeled "homeland defense" or "civil support," it is clear that the military may be the only organization within the U.S. government that has the capability to provide rapid and large-scale assistance in the early stages of a major disaster. Therefore, as planners examine potential future threats, and the realities of asymmetric warfare, it is useful to thoroughly review existing policies, procedures, operational concepts, command and control structures, force structure, force sizing, and doctrine to ensure that the United States is prepared to meet new and emerging threats.[5]

KEY INSIGHTS ON FUTURE THREATS INSIDE THE UNITED STATES

Over the course of each TRADOC-sponsored wargame, Red military planners attempted to counter the overwhelming military prowess of the U.S. military by conducting limited attacks against the United States. Recognizing that it is easier to delay, disrupt, degrade, or defeat a military force before it arrays itself for combat, all Red teams considered plans to attack the U.S. homeland. The resulting insights can be grouped into seven primary categories: asymmetric warfare, direct action attacks in the United States, the concept of a self-

---

[5]These issues were not addressed in any significant detail in any of the wargames conducted by TRADOC; however, it is important to examine all aspects of the problem. For example, should the Army specifically size and structure a portion of its force for homeland security? While this is an issue open for debate, the decision should not be made until after the potential requirements have been assessed for a range of situations, to include an adversary launching multiple attacks within the United States during the early stages of an overseas operation.

defined "redline," targeting of power-projection capabilities, deterring U.S. military action, perception management operations, and the growing incentive for preemption by future adversaries.

Asymmetric Warfare

The series of wargames described in Chapter Two were exceptionally rich and productive in developing insights about how future adversaries might choose to fight the United States. Each Red team developed a variant of a "counter–power projection" strategy to delay the arrival of the U.S. military and prevent it from using effectively its very potent capabilities as posited in the 2020 time period.[6] This overarching strategy is composed of three major operational concepts: antideployment operations actions taken primarily within the United States; antiaccess operations taken to prevent forces or capabilities from arriving in theater; and combat operations conducted in theater. Combined, these efforts were designed to alter the cost/benefit calculus associated with a potential U.S. response and, if possible, present the United States with a *fall accompli* in theater. While the specific actions undertaken by each adversary varied, the general approaches to the problem were similar. The question becomes, why have so many Red teams selected similar operational concepts?

It is clear that the results of Desert Storm, coupled with the postulated 2020 warfighting capabilities of the United States, are likely to force adversaries to seek ways to undermine U.S. strengths by developing capabilities that the United States can neither match in kind nor effectively counter. Broadly speaking, asymmetric warfare refers to the application of selected means and methods in an expressly unanticipated and nontraditional manner. In its ideal and most extreme form, asymmetric warfare causes a cascading effect that is out of proportion to the effort invested. Asymmetric approaches, therefore, often seek a major psychological impact to produce shock and

---

[6]Throughout the AAN and Army Transformation projects, as well as other research related to the emerging Revolution in Military Affairs (RMA), Red teams consistently attempted to bring the war to the United States. While there is always a danger of "Americanizing" how foreign militaries will respond to an operational and strategic problem, the fact that this approach is so common warrants continued analysis.

confusion and thereby affect the opponent's will, initiative, and freedom of action. This condition, whether it is called disruption or disorganization, in turn creates conditions whereby an inferior force can gain conventional advantage over a superior force. Such approaches are applicable at all levels of warfare—strategic, operational, and tactical—and can employ or affect one or more elements of national power. Thus, asymmetric warfare may be viewed as an attempt to circumvent or undermine an opponent's strengths while exploiting his weaknesses, using methods that differ significantly from an expected mode of operation.

This definition of asymmetric warfare highlights the fact that it is not a separate form of warfare. Rather, asymmetric warfare will likely be applied across the full range of military operations. In each of the wargames, adversaries chose to challenge the United States by employing asymmetrical counters throughout the theater of operations. What surprised many of the Blue players, however, was the willingness of adversaries to conduct military and paramilitary operations within the boundaries of the United States.[7]

One of the clearest findings to come from the TRADOC wargames and subsequent analyses is that asymmetries almost always exist in both the interests and the objectives of parties to a conflict. For instance, in many contingency operations the vital interests of the United States are not at stake, but the vital interests of the regional actors *are*. Indeed, just the deployment of U.S. forces into the area of conflict has the potential to alter the power relationships of all participants. Moreover, depending upon the particular mission, the arrival of U.S. forces could place the very survival of an organization or regime in jeopardy. If an adversary concludes that the United States is threatening the survival of its regime, an asymmetry of motivation will emerge that could result in actions that might appear irrational from the U.S. perspective—perhaps even the employment of chemical, biological, radiological, or nuclear weapons within the United States.

---

[7]Many of the Red players were, in turn, surprised that the Blue team did not expect this type of response. As expressed by one of the Red military commanders, why would a determined adversary grant the United States immunity from homeland attacks when the United States is unwilling to grant the same to him?

Direct Action Attacks within the United States

In an era where the United States has fewer forward-deployed combat forces, potential adversaries may view the U.S. homeland as an assembly area that is vulnerable to attack. In 1921, General Giulio Douhet stated that "it is easier and more effective to destroy the enemy's aerial power by destroying his nests and eggs on the ground than to hunt his flying birds in the air."[8] This same intellectual construct encouraged the Red team players to attack the United States. Indeed, each of the teams concluded that if conflict with the United States was inevitable, limited attacks within its homeland were essential. Interestingly, despite the degree to which the United States destroyed Iraq during the Persian Gulf War, the threat of massive retaliatory destruction did not keep the adversary from attacking the United States. In fact, Red teams determined that the United States would inflict massive destruction on their military forces, capabilities, and related infrastructure whether they carried out attacks within the United States or not. Consequently, they concluded that their best chance for victory depended on keeping the United States from building up forces and capabilities in the region; and the only way they could achieve that goal was to attack civilian and military targets within the United States. Furthermore, every Red team NCA chose to attack targets within the United States as a political statement signaling Red's willingness to retaliate and significantly raise the costs for U.S. policymakers.

Types of direct action attacks contemplated by the Red teams included the following:

- Chemical or biological attacks on key civilian transportation hubs, mobilization/deployment centers, and military installations used by deploying forces. These attacks would delay and degrade deployment and divert medical and decontamination resources that might normally be deployed to theater.

- Direct action attacks to damage easily accessible space and information nodes—such as the "Blue Cube" in Sunnyvale—

---

[8]General Giulio Douhet, as quoted by Alan Vick, *Snakes in the Eagle's Nest: A History of Ground Attacks on Air Bases*, Santa Monica, CA: RAND, MR-553-AF, 1995.

needed by the United States to fight the type of future war envisioned.

- Attacks on ammunition depots and ports *or* on their supporting infrastructure (e.g., transportation). Rail links leading from ammunition depots were also viewed to be especially vulnerable and lucrative targets.

- Use and/or threatened use of shoulder-fired air defense missiles against military and civilian airlift. The United States relies extensively on civilian airlift for passenger movement. These aircraft lack defensive systems. Here the psychological effects of an attack might be even more important than the physical effects, because even a miss would probably stop the deployment of U.S. forces until the threat had been eliminated. Not only did the teams conclude that this would be a likely form of attack, they also believed that it would have a staggering effect on our ability to deploy forces. Such an attack would slow the deployment sequence as well as stimulate an increase in security around all U.S. bases that would effectively cause combat forces to be "fixed in place" and thus kept out of the theater.

- Employment of a radiological agent using a high-explosive device to disseminate a contaminant during the deployment process. Players believed that such a weapon would have the residual effect of a nuclear weapon on equipment (e.g., all aircraft and equipment at the site would be unusable for years) but would not cause a massive number of casualties.

- Attacks on fabrication facilities for critical low-density items such as cruise missiles.

- Attacks on symbolic targets such as the White House, the Pentagon, national monuments, or other symbols of American power.

- Attacks on key infrastructure targets such as electrical grids, railroad tunnels, bridges, and large dams.

The Concept of a "Redline"

While Red teams contemplated conducting attacks within the United States,[9] they were self-deterred from taking any action that might cross what one team referred to as the "redline." The concept of a redline was first raised in the 1997 Winter Wargame when the Red team leader stated that certain actions would undoubtedly trigger an unacceptable level of U.S. escalation, and might result in a determined American response to achieve a "total victory." Red team members were careful to select targets and weapons in a manner that they believed would achieve the greatest military impact without giving the United States government the moral justification necessary to seek the total destruction of the adversary.

Based upon this concept, Red team members decided to attack the U.S. military hard enough to degrade its capabilities and delay the arrival of its forces in theater but, at the same time, not cause so many casualties as to create a "Pearl Harbor effect." From the standpoint of the Red team leaders, the challenge was to seize the initiative and attack while they still had sufficient capability, but not so early as to appear to be the aggressor. Additionally, Red team leaders shied away from using "terrorist" attacks against civilian targets and, instead, conducted "direct action" attacks against militarily significant targets.[10] This is not to say that civilian targets were never attacked. Rather, the purpose of such attacks was to deter, delay, degrade, or

---

[9]Red teams concluded that war with the United States started at the moment the U.S. military began the deployment process. For international political purposes, however, several of the Red teams decided to initiate their attacks within the homeland only after the United States began its air and missile attacks. But from a military perspective, there was significant pressure to attack deploying units at the onset of the deployment process. While such attacks would appear to be preemptive from the standpoint of the United States, they were considered defensive actions by each of the adversaries.

[10]With the exception of the 1997 Summer Wargame, each Red team represented a nation-state that was susceptible to the overwhelming military power of the U.S. military. The players acknowledged that while the concept of a "redline" would probably deter an attack that could be attributable to a specific country, the actions of a terrorist organization might not be so constrained. Indeed, during the 1997 Summer Wargame the Orange team planned terrorist actions that would have caused large-scale civilian casualties. However, none of these planned attacks were adjudicated to be successful.

destroy U.S. military capabilities, not to create terror.[11] It is also important to note that many of the Red teams concluded that the "limited use" of certain chemical and biological agents would probably not cross the American "redline," although it might if the casualty count became too high. The Red objective was to conduct combat operations in the United States, not create mass casualties. Whether this assessment is correct is less important than the fact that Red team participants believed it was. The question is, will future adversaries perceive this same weakness in U.S. power projection and make the same assessments about how it can be crippled?

Counter–Power Projection Operations

Each of the Red teams chose different means to prevent, delay, or degrade the deployment of U.S. forces from CONUS. For instance, the primary goal of one of the Red teams was to delay the arrival and replenishment of U.S. forces for thirty days. This would allow sufficient time for Red forces to achieve their military objectives, and to present the United States with a *fait accompli*. To do this, the Red team leadership sought to create chaos, delay deployment, and disrupt the provision of support to deployed forces by attacking targets inside the United States. A large obstacle confronting Red in its attempt to pursue such a strategy was its limited capability to place agents inside the United States. However, given a five- or ten-year planning window, the Red team concluded that it would have had sufficient time to establish an agent network inside the United States.[12]

Given this assumption and the proclivity of many adversaries to assign multiple agents to a single target, it was further determined

---

[11]It is important to note that some actions could be defined as either terrorism or direct action, depending upon the intended purpose of the attacker. For instance, an attack on the Pentagon could be characterized as direct action if the purpose was to degrade the command and control capabilities of the U.S. military. Conversely, the same attack could be characterized as terrorism if the purpose was to create a sense of terror in the civilian populace.

[12]Each Red team included a number of military and civilian personnel who were subject matter experts on the adversary they were playing. Consequently, Red actions in the United States were viewed through the lens of an adversary who contemplated the possibility of confronting the United States sometime in the future, and then enacted plans and policies that would provide the greatest possibility of success.

that approximately thirty targets could be attacked with a high probability of success. Teams also concluded that any physical attacks in
the United States would have to be timed to coincide with the initiation of hostilities or the deployment of U.S. forces because of the
high likelihood that agents or teams would be compromised after the
beginning of hostilities. The teams also believed that these limited
"combat operations" conducted in the United States would cause a
significant competition for resources that would otherwise be deployed to fight the theater war. In essence, the Red team wanted to
open up a second front for the U.S. military—the continental United
States. Finally, all the Red teams concluded that the mere existence
of a credible threat of attack in the United States would significantly
degrade the ability of the U.S. military to move rapidly during the
deployment process, thus buying them the time necessary to achieve
their objectives in theater.

Deterring U.S. Military Action

A future adversary who acquires the capability to attack civilian and
military targets within the United States using asymmetric means
has the potential to credibly threaten attacks as a response to U.S.
deployment. During the 1997 Summer Wargame, which portrayed a
conflict where U.S. vital interests were not directly threatened, the
response of the Blue political leadership was to delay the deployment
of initial-entry special operations forces until after the perceived
threat in CONUS had been largely eliminated. Thus, having a credible capability to inflict serious damage in the U.S. homeland may
have the potential to deter U.S. military action. It should be noted
that the 1997 adversary had a large number of agents operating
within the United States who, together, had the capability to cause a
significant amount of damage and loss of life throughout the country. Several factors were at play in this decision to delay the deployment of U.S. forces. First, vital U.S. interests were not at risk.
Second, a delay of several weeks would have provided the law enforcement community with the time necessary to reduce the level of
risk within the United States. And third, the U.S. military leadership
did not believe the delay would prevent them from ultimately
achieving their objective—although it did make the tactical and operational problems more difficult.

Some may argue that any acquiescence to these types of threats allows U.S. policy to be held hostage to terrorism. However, this asymmetric operational strategy has its conceptual underpinning in conventional deterrence. Rather than being held hostage to terrorism, the United States is being deterred by a credible military threat. Simply because the military threat is not posed by missiles, bombs, or invasion by a land force does not mean that it cannot inflict great damage to lives and property. Future adversaries who do not have the technological wherewithal to fight the United States head-to-head may well consider trucks laden with high explosives, chemicals, or biological agents within the United States to be their best chance of deterring U.S. military action.

Because of the specifics of this case it would be wrong to generalize and state that threats to the United States would delay the deployment process. Although in some cases this might be the result, many U.S. administrations have shown themselves to be remarkably unmoved by potential threats. That being said, however, depending upon the circumstances it is a potential that must be considered.

Perception Management Operations

The key to a successful campaign against the United States may be a well-developed perception management effort. Indeed, Red team participants noted that a carefully executed perception management campaign was a critically important component of their strategy to defeat the United States. Perception management can be effectively used to shape how a population and relevant political support groups view given aspects of an operation. Although perception management is an important tool for all nations, democratic countries are especially vulnerable to this form of information warfare because of the openness of their societies. The effective use of modern communications and media technologies may enable other governments, factions, or splinter groups to counter U.S. military superiority in the theater of operations by targeting U.S. and coalition populations with symbolic images, events, and propaganda designed to undercut support for the operation. Further, potential competitors may use disinformation, propaganda, and agitation to destroy U.S. and coalition legitimacy.

Future opponents might conclude that because American political culture equates democracy with unfettered public discourse, all sides to a conflict will be given equal time to present their case to the American people. Moreover, because of the critical posture adopted by the media and the public toward political figures, the American people have become more likely to view information disseminated by the U.S. government with skepticism. For instance, U.S. military attempts to restrict media access in Grenada, Panama, and Operation Desert Shield/Storm were widely criticized by the media as interference with their ability to collect information independent of official sources. Thus, the U.S. government is at an inherent disadvantage when countering perception management operations, especially in parts of the world such as the Middle East, Asia, and Latin America where U.S. motivations are held suspect by an overwhelmingly large portion of the population. Conversely, adversaries are free to say and do whatever they please. Indeed, it is not uncommon for foreign governments to hire public relations firms to try to ensure that their message is effectively reaching the public and relevant special interest groups within the United States and the international community.[13] This is not to say that opponents get better press within the United States, but rather that they get a fair press; that is not often the case for the U.S. government in many parts of the world.

Incentives for Preemptive Attacks

One of the most striking observations to come from the wargames is the magnitude of the incentive that potential adversaries have to conduct preemptive attacks against the United States. Given America's overwhelming conventional power-projection capabilities,

---

[13]One of the most publicized examples of this occurred during the 1980s, when the Sandinista-led government of Nicaragua employed a very effective propaganda and public relations effort to undercut the Reagan Administration's policy. Elements of this perception management campaign were aimed at special interest groups, religious organizations, the media, the general public, and members of the United States Congress and the international diplomatic community. Although the Reagan Administration attempted to counter this through the creation of the office of "Public Diplomacy," these efforts were largely ineffective. See Richard R. Brennan, Jr., *The Concept of "Type C" Coercive Diplomacy: U.S. Policy Towards Nicaragua During the Reagan Administration*, Ph.D. Dissertation, University of California at Los Angeles, 1999, pp. 207–216.

game participants concluded that future adversaries could not afford to permit the United States to mobilize and deploy forces to theater. Therefore, several Red teams concluded that certain critical nodes would have to be attacked either before or immediately after the onset of hostilities. Targets for preemptive action included logistics infrastructure, command and control sites, space assets, selected airfields, ammunition storage sites, seaports, and airports. The political leadership of the Red teams wrestled with the issue of timing: attempting to balance the political gain generated from allowing the United States to initiate hostile actions against the perceived military need to delay and degrade the arrival of U.S. forces.

While this concept is not altogether new, the discussion by Red planning staffs highlighted the fact that a future opponent, by attacking a relatively small number of carefully chosen targets, could significantly degrade U.S. warfighting capabilities.[14] In addition, the Red teams concluded that by striking first at multiple high-value targets they could establish a credible threat of future, large-scale escalation.[15] Indeed, one of the teams concluded that by establishing a credible threat of being willing and able to conduct a WMD attack in the United States, an adversary might be able to deter certain U.S. military actions against targets located in Red population centers.

EMERGING ISSUES

While a number of important homeland security insights have emerged from the AAN and ATWG projects, it is clear that there re-

---

[14]One Red team concluded that chemical attacks using persistent agents at Fort Campbell Army Airfield, Robert Gray Army Airfield, Hunter Army Airfield, and Pope Air Force Base would cripple the rapid-deployment capability of the Army. The impact would be amplified if similar actions were taken at a small number of seaports located on the East Coast and Gulf of Mexico (e.g., Bayonne, Savannah, Charleston, Beaumont, and Galveston) and large Air Force bases (e.g., McGuire, Dover, Langley, Charleston, and Seymore Johnson).

[15]Red teams generally concluded that the U.S. nuclear arsenal was virtually useless during conventional warfare. Therefore, nuclear escalation by the United States was never seriously contemplated. While there was uncertainty about whether the United States would respond to a large-scale chemical or biological attack by retaliating with nuclear weapons, most participants concluded that nuclear weapons were off-limits to U.S. policymakers except in the event of large-scale, indiscriminate civilian casualties.

main many more questions than answers. Moreover, because of the nature of the problem, many of these issues are bigger than the Army. The following issues were raised during "national policy team" deliberations by wargame participants who were role-playing senior government officials such as the President, Secretary of State, Secretary of Defense, Attorney General, and so forth. Although sufficient analysis was not conducted during the wargames to develop findings or conclusions, these issues were the subject of debate and require further study.

Blurred Line Between Law Enforcement and Military Operations

Homeland security tends to blur the line between law enforcement and military operations, causing conflict and confusion over an appropriate response. For example, if an enemy infantry brigade were conducting operations within the United States, there would be little doubt that the U.S. military would be responsible for eliminating the threat. However, what happens when the United States is unable to identify the source of a particular threat? Are the incidents state directed, or the result of nonstate terrorism? What happens when enemy SOF teams are known to be located within the United States and are prepared to take hostile action? Clearly, an attack on U.S. critical infrastructure or command and control sites such as the Pentagon could be considered either an act of terrorism or an act of war. At what point does a hostile act cross the line from a crime to a national security threat? Is the situation different if the threat is generated from covert agents? Some have argued that the presence of any enemy units on American territory would result in a declaration of war, at which point extraordinary civil-military measures would be justified. But if we are using our military to locate and destroy small enemy units within the United States, then what impact is that having on our ability to prosecute a war overseas? Finally, what happens if some U.S. civilians are cooperating with the foreign units or agents?

An associated issue relates to the employment of national collection assets within the continental United States. At what point might it be appropriate to employ these national technical means to identify, locate, and potentially target enemy agents and special operations forces operating within the United States? While statutory authority is set forth in 10 U.S.C. 382, is it sufficient to handle new and emerging threats? What is the proper lash-up between the Department of Defense, the Department of Justice, and the judiciary in these situations? How do we protect the United States in these situations without undermining our core values?

Extent of Impact on the Deployment Process

During each of the wargames, the assessment cell attempted to calculate the effect that attacks on the homeland would have on the deployment process. It was asserted that such attacks would disrupt the deployment process only temporarily, but very little was done to examine the second- and third-order consequences. What is the real impact of being attacked with a chemical, biological, radiological, or nuclear weapon at a power-projection facility or hub? How might deploying forces, and their home stations, prepare for such incidents to reduce the consequences of such attacks? This question was partially examined in the Pope/Bragg Study of 1998 that assessed issues associated with installation preparedness for WMD attacks.[16] The report concluded that a relatively small chemical attack at Fort Bragg and Pope Air Force Base during a deployment could delay the process for more than four days because of the number of casualties and the problems associated with decontamination of both aircraft and equipment. This delay would be even longer if alternative capabilities and resources were unavailable. The report further concludes, "This delay could disrupt the programmed flow of U.S. rapid deployment forces and compromise their ability to counter threats in regions vital to U.S. interests."[17] This is, however, little more than an assertion that has not yet been quantified. To what extent could the military deployment of the United States be disrupted by relatively small attacks within the homeland? How might the effects of these attacks be mitigated?

---

[16] *Assessment of the Impact of Chemical and Biological Weapons on Joint Operations at Aerial Ports of Embarkation in 2010*, Booz-Allen & Hamilton, October 1998.

[17] Pope/Bragg Study, p. ES-3.

Consolidation versus Dispersion

If CONUS is no longer a sanctuary, then all facets of basing and deployment must be reexamined. In an effort to become more efficient, there is a growing trend toward consolidation of like units and capabilities. This trend is obvious at ammunition depots, transportation hubs, communication hubs, and even Army installations. It is also evident in war-supporting industries and product distribution centers. For instance, the large majority of Army combat personnel and equipment are located in a very small number of installations. The same phenomenon is true for the Navy, Marine Corps, and Air Force. In fact, like units tend to be grouped together to gain a higher degree of efficiency in training and maintaining the force during times of peace. Unfortunately, these large installations, depots, and hubs also create lucrative and easily identifiable targets during times of conflict.

To increase security in a high-threat environment, military units are frequently dispersed to ensure that the entire force is not placed at risk at the same time. If DoD does not want to change its current structural approach of consolidation, perhaps processes and procedures can be modified to gain greater security. For instance, during the deployment process, a large number of personnel and equipment are staged at marshalling areas in order to move personnel and equipment as quickly as possible. Should deployment processes and procedures limit the number of personnel, and the amount of equipment, massed in one area? What steps can be taken to best manage the competition between efficiency and security? This negative aspect of consolidation should be fully addressed in any future Base Realignment and Closing (BRAC) discussion.

Competition for Resources

During the first three AAN wargames, participants attempted to determine what impact enemy attacks within the United States would have on the availability of U.S. combat units and other military resources needed to fight and win a war in a distant theater.[18] The

---

[18]Given the historical precedent of the Gulf War, it is unlikely that National Guard combat elements will deploy early. More important, the use of the National Guard in

reality is that U.S. military organizations that may be called upon to support homeland security have a primary warfighting mission. Consequently, there is a danger that some of these units could have competing requirements during times of conflict, and recent Army decisions on the employment of the National Guard only increase that risk.

During the wargames, the large majority of military participants seemed to believe that incidents in the United States would *not* have a detrimental effect on their ability to deploy combat forces overseas. However, in the 1998 Spring Wargame, the Blue President directed elements of Delta Force, Task Force 160, and other elements of the JSOC to remain in the United States. The Blue CJCS was surprised that these forces were even being considered for employment within the United States. The fact was, given the threat portrayed in the wargame, that protecting the homeland became a primary concern for the U.S. political leadership. Moreover, while these missions may not neatly fall within the traditional roles and missions of the military, no other organization has the broad range of capabilities that can quickly be brought to bear to respond to this type of threat.

In the event of a successful attack by enemy forces, certain low-density units such as military police, medical, chemical decontamination, etc. may be needed in the United States until local civilian authorities can cope with the situation. Thus, from the standpoint of capabilities and resources, CINC Americas may need to fight a war in the United States—a war where the lives and property of American citizens are being directly threatened. In this situation it is at least plausible to conclude that the NCA would decide that the first priority of a portion of the U.S. military should be to protect Americans here in the United States. At a minimum, such a scenario would cause resource competition for dual-missioned units—especially those with unique skills and capabilities needed to support civilian agencies. Consequently, it is important to assess the actual and potential competition for military resources—personnel, units, and

---

its Title 32 or "state" status for homeland security missions could avoid the perceived issue of Posse Comitatus—even if the nature of the adversary were ambiguous or if it was being assisted by U.S. citizens. For these and other reasons, many are now looking at the National Guard as a key source of support for homeland security missions.

equipment—that is likely to occur if the United States is facing attacks on its homeland while simultaneously prosecuting a war overseas. To what extent could this competition for resources hinder the ability of the United States to prosecute a war overseas? What options exist that might mitigate the effect of this competition for resources—especially for high-demand/low-density personnel and units?

Organization for Homeland Security

Starting with the 1998 Spring Wargame, significant emphasis was placed on examining organizational issues associated with homeland security. The overarching concept for all these deliberations was that both American law and the American way of life mandate a strong civilian law enforcement presence within the homeland security framework. All homeland security teams understood that both politically and culturally, Americans are averse to empowering the military to play an active enforcement role within the United States.[19] Intuitively, participants concluded that the scope and duration of direct military involvement in response to attacks on the homeland would be constrained. Further, there was consensus that the Department of Defense must be prepared to do more than simply support civilian efforts. Consequently, participants struggled with developing an organizational structure—and associated processes and procedures—that would enable the United States to employ military forces and capabilities in the homeland when required but do so in a way that is consistent with American culture, laws, and Constitutional protections.[20]

---

[19]It should be noted that until September 11, 2001, the United States had not endured a real wartime attack on its homeland since the Civil War. It would be a mistake to conclude that Americans would oppose expanded military involvement in homeland security within the context of major attacks threatening significant loss of life or property damage inside the United States. A plausible argument can be made that if safety of life and property were significantly threatened, the public would welcome or even demand an expanded military role.

[20]Some may argue that this concern is only germane when dealing with terrorism, and maybe not even then. The issue is so politically sensitive, however, that cooperative military/civilian training for counterterrorism is virtually nonexistent. While statutes and directives may be in existence that authorize military forces to conduct operations within the United States, operational planning and training for such an employment

The organizational chart presented earlier (Figure 1) was an attempt by participants in the 1998 Summer Wargame to portray the linkage—and subordination—of the Department of Defense to the Department of Justice during homeland defense "combat" operations. It is important to note that there is currently a close relationship between certain elements of DoD and DOJ with regard to counterterrorism, especially with respect to weapons of mass destruction. Terrorism is a crime, however, so the rules governing the identification, apprehension, and conviction of criminals must apply at all stages of the operation. The question emerges: How does this relationship change if and when "warfare" is brought to the mainland of the United States?

It would be an exaggeration to state that the wargames and workshops sponsored by TRADOC have developed any significant insights into how local, state, and federal government agencies should organize to confront these emerging threats. While both U.S. law and the American way of life mandate a strong civilian presence within the homeland security framework, it is necessary to examine conditions where the Department of Defense might be directed to take a more prominent role in protecting the homeland. Under what conditions would the military be asked to take a more direct and prominent role in homeland security? What are the training and doctrine implications of such a role? This issue must, however, be explored before the first attack occurs; otherwise the United States is likely to be surprised and caught unprepared to either prevent or respond effectively to the attack.

Are Legislative Changes Required?

One question that must be addressed is whether existing laws are adequate for the types of threats raised in this report.[21] This assessment is predicated on the conclusion that future adversaries are

---

of forces is generally eschewed. Whatever command and control structure is adopted for this mission should be exercised on a routine basis to ensure its utility.

[21]The limitations imposed by Posse Comitatus do not exist during a declared war of national emergency. In every wargame, forces were deployed without a formal declaration of war. Moreover, the President in each of the games decided not to declare a national emergency precisely because he did not want to initiate the type of actions that such a declaration would likely require.

likely to employ terrorism or asymmetric attacks to compete militarily with the United States[22] and, further, that these attacks would overwhelm the capabilities of law enforcement and other emergency response capabilities—thus requiring the direct involvement of U.S. military forces. The question is, to what extent do existing statutes allow or proscribe U.S. military involvement within the territorial boundaries of the United States?[23]

At first blush, these types of operations appear to be outside the purview of the U.S. military. However, there are Constitutional and statutory bases for employing the military for domestic purposes.[24] Note that Article IV of the Constitution *requires* the federal government to take all necessary action to protect the several States from both invasion and domestic violence. Based upon this requirement, the military has frequently been used for domestic purposes, including taking actions designed to enforce the law.

As a result of actions taken by the military in the post–Civil War Reconstruction era, Congress passed the Posse Comitatus Act of 1878 as a broad proscription against soldiers enforcing the law.[25] There

---

[22]The "Gilmore Commission" drew a similar conclusion with regard to terrorism. See Advisory Panel to Assess Domestic Response Capabilities for Terrorism Involving Weapons of Mass Destruction, *Second Annual Report to the President and the Congress: Toward a National Strategy for Combating Terrorism*, December 15, 2000, p. C-8.

[23]Wargame participants raised the issue of Posse Comitatus each time the national policy team considered employing the military inside the United States. On every occasion, however, the Attorney General stated that the restrictions of Posse Comitatus would not prevent a president from being able to employ DoD forces and capabilities to confront a foreign threat operating inside the United States during times of conflict.

[24]Article II of the Constitution states that "The President shall be Commander in Chief of the Army and the Navy of the United States, and of the Militia of the several States, when called into the Actual Service of the United States." In addition, Article IV states that the United States "shall protect each [State] against Invasions; and on application of the Legislature, or of the executive (when the Legislature cannot be convened) against domestic violence." Finally, Article I of the Constitution provides that Congress has the authority to "make rules for the Government and Regulation of land and naval forces" and "to provide for calling forth the militia to execute the Laws of the Union, suppress Insurrections and repel Invasions."

[25]The Posse Comitatus Act, 18 U.S.C. 1385, states: "Whoever, except in the cases and under circumstances expressly authorized by the Constitution or Act of Congress, willfully uses any part of the Army or the Air Force as a posse comitatus or otherwise to execute the laws shall be fined not more than $10,000 or imprisoned not more than

are, however, numerous exceptions to the original prohibitions of Posse Comitatus, including statutes permitting counterdrug assistance, disaster relief, counterterrorism involving weapons of mass destruction, and the suppressions of insurrections and rebellions.[26]

The 1991 Defense Authorization Act contained provisions authorizing the Army to provide equipment, training, and expert advice to assist law enforcement in counterdrug operations.[27] In addition, this legislation allowed the U.S. military to provide a wide range of support to state and federal law enforcement agencies while conducting operations along the borders of the United States. This statute, however, specifically precludes military personnel from conducting activities involving search, seizure, arrest, and similar functions.

The second major exception to Posse Comitatus relates to the utilization of military forces and capabilities to assist in disaster relief. The Robert T. Stafford Disaster Relief Act of 1984 authorizes the President to employ federal military forces and capabilities following a natural disaster at the request of a state governor or legislature, and the declaration of a state of emergency by the President. Once an emergency is declared, federal forces can be used under the direction of the Federal Emergency Management Agency (FEMA).[28]

In 1988, the Congress enacted legislation allowing the military to provide equipment and other support to help law enforcement conduct counterterrorism operations. Furthermore, 10 U.S.C. 382 specifically authorizes military personnel to conduct searches, seizures, and arrests during "emergency situations involving a bio-

---

two years, or both." An amendment was passed in 1956 to add the Air Force to this legislation. According to *Black's Law Dictionary*, Posse Comitatus means, "the power or force of the country."

[26]For a more comprehensive analysis of the legal aspects of using the military for domestic purposes, see Thomas R. Lujan, "Legal Aspects of Domestic Employment of the Army," *Parameters*, Autumn 1997, pp. 82–97, and *Second Annual Report to the President and the Congress: Toward a National Strategy for Combating Terrorism*, pp. 27–28 and Annex R.

[27]10 U.S.C. 124, 371–378, and 382.

[28]42 U.S.C. 5170, 5170b, and 5191, more commonly known as the Stafford Act. See also Executive Order 12673, dated March 23, 1989, DoD Directive 3025.1, and Army Regulation 500-60.

logical or chemical weapon of mass destruction" when such threats exceed the capacity of civilian law enforcement and the special capabilities of DoD are required.[29] A similar exception to Posse Comitatus also exists for incidents involving nuclear terrorism.[30]

The fourth exception to Posse Comitatus provides broad powers allowing the President to employ federal military forces for the suppression of insurrections and rebellions and the protection of the states against domestic violence. Indeed, contrary to beliefs commonly held by many Army officers, the President has both the constitutional and statutory authority to use federal forces to maintain domestic tranquility. For example, legislation specifically states that, following a request from a state governor or legislature, the President may "call into Federal Service such of the militia of the other States, and use such of the armed forces, *as he considers necessary* to enforce the laws and suppress the rebellion." More important, the statute makes it clear that such presidential authority is "plenary," meaning it is not subject to judicial review.[31] Thus, military commanders on the ground during the Los Angeles riots of 1992 erred when they stated that federal troops and federalized members of the Army National Guard could not undertake law enforcement missions. In this situation, pursuant to presidential power to quell domestic violence, U.S. military personnel were exempt from the provisions of Posse Comitatus. This misunderstanding on the part of the JTF Commander seriously undermined the military's capability to support local law enforcement agencies.[32] How much worse could the situation have been had the military been called upon to respond to attacks, conducted by small groups of people, at numerous locations across the United States?

Are the statutory exceptions to Posse Comitatus sufficient? First, it should be noted that the President's statutory authority to employ federal forces to maintain domestic tranquility during an insurrection or rebellion is reactive in nature. Indeed, before such action can

---

[29]10 U.S.C. 382, Emergency Situations Involving Chemical or Biological Weapons of Mass Destruction.

[30]10 U.S.C. 831.

[31]10 U.S.C. 331–334.

[32]Lujan, "Legal Aspects of Domestic Employment of the Army," pp. 90–92.

be taken, a state governor or legislature must request assistance and the President must declare an emergency. In essence, this provision would allow the military to be used to restore public order after an attack took place. Similarly, the statutory provisions relating to terrorist attacks involving chemical, biological, or nuclear weapons require that the Department of Justice request assistance on the ground that the threat exceeds the capabilities of law enforcement agencies. Once again, it is likely that such a request would not be made until after one or more attacks have actually occurred.

What legislative authority would be required to allow the President to employ military forces to *prevent* asymmetric attacks in the United States? In protecting the Constitutional rights and freedoms of Americans, what command and control relationships should govern the employment of these forces? What type of training and exercises should be conducted to ensure that military forces are integrated into the broader local, state, and federal civilian response? Should, on such an exceptional basis, DoD be designated as the "lead federal agency?" These hard questions need to be examined and addressed before the first asymmetric attack in the United States. If not, they will have to be answered while the President is confronting a national emergency, the likes of which have not been encountered since the Cuban Missile Crisis.[33]

Finally, it is important to recall that, by definition, asymmetric attacks seek to undermine an opponent's strengths while exploiting his weaknesses, using methods that differ significantly from an expected mode of operation. Consequently, if the United States can anticipate and prepare for such attacks, the likelihood that they will succeed will be greatly diminished. Unfortunately, none of this will be possible without adequate enabling legislation.

---

[33]The terrorist attacks against the World Trade Center and the Pentagon on September 11 created such an emergency. In the aftermath of this attack it remains imperative that new policies, procedures, and organizational relationships be put into place in anticipation of future incidents.

Chapter Four

CONCLUSIONS ON HOMELAND SECURITY ISSUES

The central question raised by the foregoing insights and issues is this: How should the Army organize, train, and equip to defend America from asymmetric attacks conducted on U.S. soil? Can law enforcement be expected to counter a military threat? If this is a mission for the Army, are the selected units properly organized, trained, and equipped to meet the threat given the constraints associated with conducting "combat" operations within the homeland? How might the Army work in conjunction with law enforcement in such a situation?

This mission is not the exclusive responsibility of either law enforcement or the Department of Defense—it is the responsibility of both, working together with numerous other federal, state, and local agencies. Because it falls between institutional lines of authority, it is an issue that unfortunately may not be examined until *after* an event occurs that conclusively proves a need for change. The United States has a long history of waiting for an event to occur before taking actions that could prevent disasters. One need only think about Beirut, Khobar Towers, Mogadishu, USS *Cole*, and September 11 to understand the effect of asymmetric attacks. All of these tragedies might have been prevented had we been better prepared. In each case, signs and warnings were available but were not acted upon.

As discussed earlier, a growing body of literature suggests that future nation-state adversaries will employ asymmetric attacks in an attempt to deter and degrade the U.S. military or to affect U.S. public opinion and response. If this is the case, some future adversary is likely to attack the United States during times of conflict to deter, degrade, disrupt, delay, or destroy U.S. forces before they can arrive in theater. If successful, these attacks could cause the United States serious problems in the next military conflict or other military operation. Even if only partially successful, such attacks would not only significantly complicate the deployment process, but probably result in the loss of American military and civilian lives.

Stewardship requires the Army to examine its potential roles and missions in all facets of homeland security—from preventing attacks to helping civil authorities respond to the consequences of such attacks. While the Army is more comfortable with the latter, it cannot and should not avoid the former. What does it mean for the Army to prevent attacks within the United States? What organizations have this responsibility? Under what circumstances will the Army be called upon? Under whose command will Army personnel and units "fight" in America? These are not easy questions, but they are questions that must be addressed.

In 1948, UN Secretary-General Dag Hammarskjöld stated that "Peacekeeping is not a job for soldiers, but only a soldier can do it."[1] Similarly, homeland security is not exclusively a job for the Army, but perhaps only the Army can perform some of the missions most effectively.

---

[1]Cited in Army Field Manual FM 100-23, *Peace Operations*, December 1994, p. 1.

Chapter Five

INTEGRATING HOMELAND SECURITY INTO THE ARMY TRANSFORMATION GAMES

From the inception of the Army After Next Project through the current Army Transformation Study, Wargames, and Analysis Project, homeland security has been a secondary or tertiary area of interest for TRADOC. After playing a large role in the 1998 Spring Wargame, homeland security was intentionally downplayed to ensure that this issue area did not interfere with the examination of the primary research questions. The outcome of this decision has been an underestimation of the effect that homeland security will have on future operations.

Regardless of the issues explored in the Army wargaming process, it is probable that future adversaries will challenge deploying units here in the United States in an attempt to deter, disrupt, delay, degrade, or defeat the U.S. military before it ever gets to the theater of operations.[1] The United States is likely to become a second theater of operations, taxing Army resources.[2] Consequently, as the Army continues to explore issues associated with its transformation to the future force, the study of homeland security must be given a more prominent role.

The question remains: How can we examine homeland security and, simultaneously, new operational and organizational concepts asso-

---

[1]See Joint Strategic Review 1999 (JSR 99) for an analysis of asymmetric approaches to counter U.S. power-projection capabilities.

[2]The same could be said for Air Force transport resources, including civilian contract aircraft, which are likely to be diverted to the United States during large-scale consequence management operations.

ciated with future warfare overseas? Clearly, if the 1998 Spring Wargame is an indication, homeland security has the potential to dominate game play. While this may approximate reality, it does not serve the broader goals of the Army transformation process. Developing a parallel process for examining issues associated with homeland security can solve this problem. Such an effort might entail the establishment of an annual workshop, inclusion of a homeland security team in the annual Army Transformation Wargame, and then a "replay" of certain aspects during a homeland security wargame.[3]

The purpose of the homeland security workshop would be to identify and prioritize questions and issues to be examined. The workshop would also be used to develop operational or organizational concepts that would then be used as strawmen during the conduct of both the Army Transformation Wargame and the homeland security wargame. Of particular interest would be the assessment of the ability of the Army's future Objective Force to employ its full-spectrum capabilities in homeland security missions. Finally, the workshop would be used as a venue for identifying key homeland security participants for the upcoming wargames.

During the TRADOC-sponsored wargame, a homeland security team would be established to serve as subject matter experts for both Blue and Red. In addition to helping the respective teams better understand issues associated with homeland security game play, the homeland security team will become familiar with how both Red and Blue intended to conduct operations in the United States. The homeland security team would also assist the assessment cell in adjudicating events that occur within the United States. Finally, issues associated with homeland security should be explicitly addressed by the Blue policy team prior to game play.

Following the Army Transformation Wargame, TRADOC should organize and conduct a homeland security wargame. This wargame

---

[3]Having said this, we should not artificially insulate the transformation game from homeland security issues just to permit unconstrained focus on the forward battle. If this is allowed to occur, the Army is not likely to learn anything useful. If homeland security adversely affects Blue play, then we have learned that there is something wrong with the way we are proposing to fight. The answer should not be to simply assume the problem away.

would replay certain actions taken during the transformation game, but focus on the homeland security component of the exercise. The purpose of this endeavor would be to measure the impact that enemy activities in the United States might have on various aspects of power-projection operations. The results of this wargame could then be incorporated into the annual report prepared by TRADOC. The process identified above would enable the study of homeland security to be integrated into the broader study of future war being conducted under the auspices of the Army Transformation Study, Wargames, and Analysis Project. By maintaining a focus on the long-term future, this process would also allow the Army to examine issues that would be difficult to address in the context of current operations. This may well be the only way the nation can prepare to meet the new and emerging threats that have been identified in this paper.

BIBLIOGRAPHY

Advisory Panel to Assess Domestic Response Capabilities for Terrorism Involving Weapons of Mass Destruction, *First Annual Report to the President and the Congress: Toward a National Strategy for Combating Terrorism*, December 1999.

Advisory Panel to Assess Domestic Response Capabilities for Terrorism Involving Weapons of Mass Destruction, *Second Annual Report to the President and the Congress: Toward a National Strategy for Combating Terrorism*, December 15, 2000.

Army After Next Project, *Report to the Chief of Staff of the Army*, Fort Monroe, VA: TRADOC, June 1996.

Army After Next 1997 Summer Wargame, *Domestic Counterterrorism Workshop Briefing Book*, Science Applications International Corporation, June 1997.

Army After Next 1997 Summer Wargame, *Domestic Counterterrorism Team Notebook*, Doctrine Directorate, Fort Monroe, VA: TRADOC, September 1997.

Army After Next 1997 Summer Wargame, *Senior Leader Seminar Briefing Book*, Fort Monroe, VA: TRADOC, September 18, 1997.

Army After Next 1998 Spring Wargame, *Senior Leader Seminar Briefing Book*, Fort Monroe, VA: TRADOC, April 30, 1998.

Army After Next 1998 Spring Wargame, *Reference Book Volume I and II*, Fort Monroe, VA: TRADOC, April 1998.

Brennan, Richard R., Jr., *The Concept of "Type C" Coercive Diplomacy: U.S. Policy Towards Nicaragua During the Reagan Administration*, Ph.D. Dissertation, University of California at Los Angeles, 1999.

Burshnick, Lieutenant General Anthony J., et al., *Assessment of the Impact of Chemical and Biological Weapons on Joint Operations at Aerial Ports of Embarkation in 2010*, Short title: "Pope/Bragg Study," Falls Church, VA: Booz-Allen & Hamilton, October 1998. Unclassified/Limited Distribution.

Foss, General John W., General Frederick J. Kroesen, et al., *Assessment of the Impact of Chemical and Biological Weapons on Joint Operations in 2010*, Falls Church, VA: Booz-Allen & Hamilton, December 1, 1997. Not available to the public.

Foss, General John W., General Frederick J. Kroesen, et al., *Assessment of the Impact of Chemical and Biological Weapons on Joint Operations in 2010: A Summary Report*, Short title: "CB 2010 Study," Falls Church, VA: Booz-Allen & Hamilton, November 1997. Unclassified/Limited Distribution.

Gardela, Karen, and Bruce Hoffman, *The RAND Chronology of International Terrorism for 1986*, Santa Monica, CA: RAND, R-3890-RC, 1990.

Larson, Eric V., and John E. Peters, *Preparing the U.S. Army to Meet Future Threats to the Homeland*, Santa Monica, CA: RAND, MR-1251-A 2000.

Lujan, Thomas R., "Legal Aspects of Domestic Employment of the Army," *Parameters*, Autumn 1997, pp. 82–97.

Perry, Walter L., and Marc Dean Millot, *Issues from the 1997 Army After Next Winter Wargame*, Santa Monica, CA: RAND, MR-988-A, 1998.

Perry, Walter L., Bruce R. Pirnie, and John Gordon IV, *Issues Raised During the Army After Next Spring Wargame*, Santa Monica, CA: RAND, MR-1023-A, 1999.

Vick, Alan, *Snakes in the Eagle's Nest: A History of Ground Attacks on Air Bases*, Santa Monica, CA: RAND, MR-553-AF, 1995.

United States Army Maneuver Support Center, "Memorandum from the Homeland Security Office to the Commander, USA Training and Doctrine Command, Subject: Homeland Security Army After Next Game Results," July 27, 2000.

United States Army, *Army Homeland Security (HLS) Strategic Planning Guidance: Coordinating Draft*, Office of the Deputy Chief of Staff for Operations, Headquarters, Department of the Army, September 10, 2001.